cool Cat DoODLES

by Deborah Zemke

BLUE APPLE

Acrocat

All cats are born acrobats! They jump, flip, twirl, whirl, and always land on their feet.

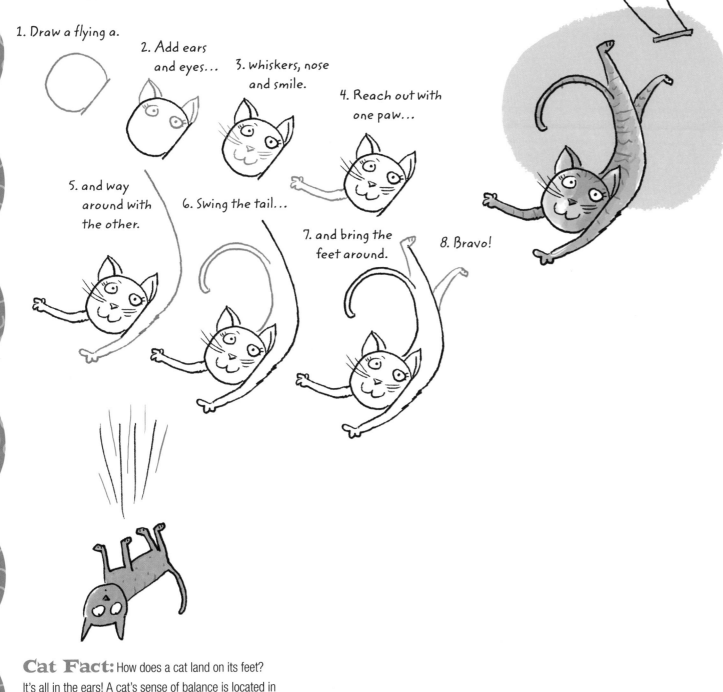

1. Draw a flying a.

2. Add ears and eyes...

3. whiskers, nose and smile.

4. Reach out with one paw...

5. and way around with the other.

6. Swing the tail...

7. and bring the feet around.

8. Bravo!

Cat Fact: How does a cat land on its feet? It's all in the ears! A cat's sense of balance is located in its inner ear and automatically lets a cat know whether it's upside down or right side up, falling or flying.

Bobcat Ballerina

On your toes! All cats, including the wild bobcat, walk on their toes. They can do this because they have long toes—and long feet. What looks to us like a cat's foot is mostly its toes, and what seems like a knee or elbow is its foot.

1. Draw a b.

2. Turn it into an uplifted paw.

3. Make a ballerina face.

4. Add four curves...

5. an outstretched paw...

6. and a tutu.

7. Draw one leg on pointe...

8. and another leg bent.

9. Tie on ballet slippers.

Hi, my name is Bob. Bob Cat.

Curious Calico

Cats are explorers and hunters. They're always looking and listening for something interesting. What's that sound? Was that a mouse?

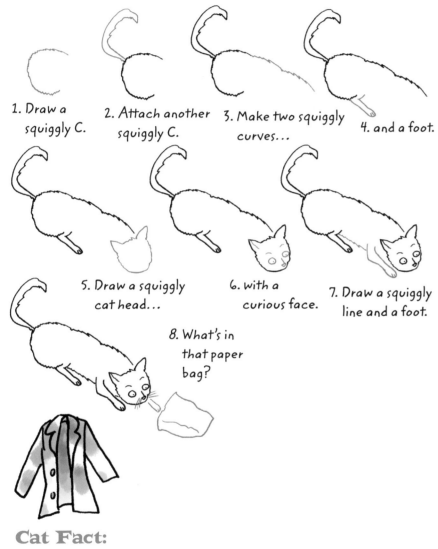

1. Draw a squiggly C.

2. Attach another squiggly C.

3. Make two squiggly curves...

4. and a foot.

5. Draw a squiggly cat head...

6. with a curious face.

7. Draw a squiggly line and a foot.

8. What's in that paper bag?

Cat Fact:

It's a coat of many colors! Calico cats are white with patches of two other colors, usually orange tabby and black. And don't call a calico cat Tom, because they're always female.

Dancing Dragon Li

This real cat is named after a mythical dragon. For hundreds of years, the Dragon Li cat has been a household pet in China, where dragons are symbols of good luck and strength.

1. Draw a D.

2. Add eyes, nose...

3. ears and whiskers.

4. Draw two squiggly, bent arms...

5. with paws and claws.

6. Draw two spiky curves.

7. Add a curve and a paw with claws.

8. Make a spiky tail...

9. and dance!

Cat Fact:

Don't mess with this cat! When a cat is ready to attack, the hair along its spine and tail stands up.

Egyptian Mau

Symbols of beauty and grace, cats were so loved in ancient Egypt that they were mummified like humans. Cats weren't just pretty pets. They earned their place by keeping their households free of rats and cobras. The modern Egyptian Mau takes its name from the ancient word *mau*, meaning cat.

1. Draw two sideways e's.

2. Add cat ears and a squarish face.

3. Make a nose and mouth.

4. Draw a big curve ending in a loop.

5. Add one curve...

6. and another curve.

7. Make front paws...

8. spots and stripes.

Ancient Egyptians wrote with a picture alphabet called hieroglyphics. Can you read what this says?

Fur Fashionista

Long or short? Cream, brown, red, or lilac? Colored tips or solid blue? Spotted, striped or tortoiseshell, cats wear coats of many colors and lengths.

Solid   Tipped   Smoke   Ticked

1. Draw a stylish f.

2. Make two eyes and ears...

3. a nose, mouth and furry cheeks.

4. Add a stylish hat and whiskers.

5. Put one paw on her hip...

6. and one paw in the air.

7. Draw a swinging skirt...

8. and two legs with little white boots.

9. Add a fancy tail, spots and stripes.

Gigacat

Giga is big, as in a billion times big! The heaviest domestic cat on record weighed almost 47 pounds, but most domestic cats weigh between 5 and 12 pounds.

1. Draw a big G.

2. Add a little nose and whiskers.

3. Make eyes and ears.

4. Draw a big, squiggly curve on one side...

5. and another on the other side.

6. Add two little feet...

7. two more feet, and a tail.

Kitty Quiz:

What kitty plays baseball?

The cat-cher.

1. Draw a sideways h.

2. Make a curled tail...

3. and an outstretched paw.

4. Attach a curve with an ear.

5. Draw another ear and paw.

6. Add wide open eyes and whiskers...

7. and coast over the countryside.

Hovercat

Cats like to have a bird's-eye view. When they're up high, they can see what's going on, whether any mice are scampering by. If cats could actually fly like this Hovercat, mice might never be able to come out of their holes!

Kitty Quiz:

What's a cat's favorite hobby?

Birdwatching.

Ice Skater

Cats are sure-footed creatures with tough foot pads that allow them to walk on snow and ice without putting their boots on.

1. Draw a cursive i.

2. Add eyes and ears…

3. head and hat.

4. Draw four curves…

5. two mittens, and whiskers.

6. Draw a top…

7. and a skirt.

8. Draw four curves…

9. two ice skates, and a tail.

Cat Fact: As a cat's claw grows, the cat needs to sharpen it by removing the old layers. Scratching on the furniture is how a cat gives herself a manicure.

Jazz Cat

Listen to this cool cat blow his horn! The largest wild cat in the Western Hemisphere, the jaguar fishes, swims, climbs trees, and roars.

1. Draw a J.

2. Add two rounded ears...

3. and sunglasses.

4. Puff up and hold out a paw...

5. to hold the horn.

6. Puff up some more...

7. on two feet.

8. Swing the tail.

9. Add spots...

10. and put this cool cat in a tree.

Cat Fact: Your cat may not roar like a jaguar, but it does...

mew PURRRRRR chirrr CATERWAUL GGRRRRRRowl snarl hissssssssssss

Kung fu Kitten

Kittens just want to have fun! As soon as a kitten is strong enough to hold its head stable and move its paws in coordination with its eyes, it's ready to play. And what is more fun than seeing a kitten pounce on a ball, leap at a leaf, or exuberantly chase nothing at all?

1. Draw a slanted K.

2. Reach out with a paw.

3. Add ears and whiskers.

4. Make a chin and elbow.

5. Add two spread-out legs...

6. paws...

7. and a tail.

Two kittens play a fierce game of imaginary volleyball.

Leaping Leopard

Look out! This big cat can jump 10 feet up and 20 feet out. Those beautiful spots help keep the leopard hidden while it waits in ambush for its passing dinner.

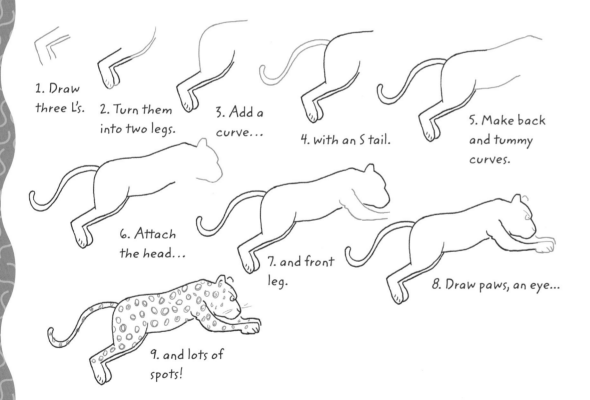

1. Draw three L's.

2. Turn them into two legs.

3. Add a curve...

4. with an S tail.

5. Make back and tummy curves.

6. Attach the head...

7. and front leg.

8. Draw paws, an eye...

9. and lots of spots!

I feel pretty in pink.

Can a leopard change its spots? This one did.

Mommy Cat

Newborn kittens need their mommy! A mother cat feeds, cleans, and completely cares for her blind, deaf, and hungry kittens. She moves them one by one to a new location if she feels they're not safe.

1. Draw M ears.

2. Add a nose, neck...

3. and cat face.

4. Put a kitten in the mouth.

5. Draw a front leg...

6. back and tummy.

7. Make a tail.

8. Draw another leg...

9. two more legs...

10. and take your kitten to a safe spot.

Food or foe?

Cat Fact: When kittens are about three weeks old, their mother teaches them to take care of themselves.

Cat Napper

Time for a nap? Yes! Cats nap almost 12 hours a day! Add about three and a half hours when they're deeply sleeping, and that leaves only eight hours each day that a cat is wide awake and ready to play or eat or....yaaaawn, isn't it time for a nap?

1. Draw a fat n.

2. Add ears and a squiggle chin.

3. Who's snoring?

4. Draw a squiggly curve...

5. and a curvy loop.

6. Make paws for pillows...

7. and a pillow.

Kitty Quiz:

What's black and white and says

Mooo-ow!

A herd of cat-tle.

Ocelot in Orbit

Ocelots are wild cats found all the way from Texas to Argentina, but not in outer space. You see spots and stripes on an ocelot—if you could see one at all, since this beautiful cat usually stays hidden in the daytime and only comes out at night.

1. Draw an O.

2. Put a cat head inside...

3. with a face.

4. Add a loop and a curved U...

5. four lines...

6. six lines...

7. gloves and boots.

8. Make a tail and planet Earth.

Cat Fact: What is that divine odor? Tuna fish three blocks away! A cat's sense of smell, or olfactory system, is three times stronger than that of a human.

Persian Princess

Long-haired Persians are popular because of their quiet, calm personalities. That makes them purrrrfect indoor pets.

1. Draw a P.

2. Add a pretty face...

3. flowers and whiskers.

4. Draw a big loop...

5. and two royal feet.

6. Add two squiggles...

7. and precious jewels.

Kitty Quiz:
What's a cat's favorite smell?

Fish oil perrrrrrrrfume.

Queen Quilt

Here, kitty, kitty, kitty. I mean, here, Your Royal Highness! If your cat acts like royalty, it's because she is! Grown female cats are called queens.

Make a Queen Quilt by turning each of the Q squares into a different cat queen and coloring the blank squares. Here's one regal idea:

Kitty Quiz:

Who's the happiest royal cat?

The Siamese em-purrer!

Robocat

This robocat is better than a mousetrap! Its ears swivel around to catch the quietest little squeak. Then it turns on the turbo to catch the mouse.

1. Draw an R.

2. Add two swivel antenna ears...

3. two glowing eyes...

4. an electronic nose and whiskers.

5. Make three buttons and a box.

6. Draw two wheels and paws...

7. and a turbo tail.

Cat Fact: Cats have 12 muscles in their ears so they can turn their ears like antennae.

Scaredy-Cat

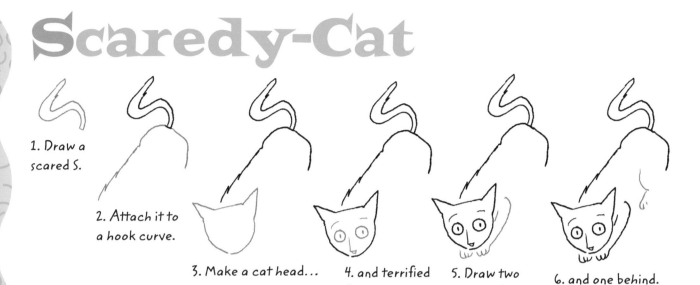

1. Draw a scared S.

2. Attach it to a hook curve.

3. Make a cat head...

4. and terrified face.

5. Draw two paws in front...

6. and one behind.

7. Put your cat up a tree!

Cats aren't afraid to scamper up a tree, but coming down is a whole other matter! That's because their curved claws are great for grabbing the tree on the way up, but not on the way down. And since their back legs are more powerful than their front, cats have more push going up. Cats need to learn how to climb down backwards.

Kitty Quiz:

What's the worst thing that can happen to a cat?

A cat-astrophe

Tea Cup Tabby

A tabby isn't a breed, but rather any cat that has a coat with spots, swirls, stripes and whirls. Classic tabbies have an M on their foreheads.

1. Draw a tiny T.

2. Add two tiny paws and a curve.

3. Make cat ears.

4. Add four curves.

5. Make two eyes and v's.

6. Draw a big curve cup...

7. and backward S tail.

8. Make a squiggly curve saucer...

9. and flowers.

Recognize this cat? The Cheshire Cat appeared in Alice in Wonderland. He also disappeared, all except for his grin! In reality, grown cats have 30 teeth, with 12 little incisors in front.

Underwater Cat

The only cat you'll ever find underwater is a catfish. Most domestic cats hate water. Why get wet and miserable and then spend the whole day getting dry again? The Turkish Van is the exception. It will jump into a lake or pool and swim around, doing a "catpaddle."

1. Draw a fat, squiggly U.

2. Attach ears and a squiggly curve.

3. Make a face.

4. Draw a furry tail and whiskers.

5. Kick with the back legs...

6. and reach with the front paws...

7. for a fish...

8. or two or three or five!

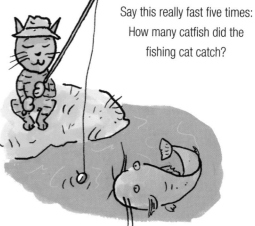

Say this really fast five times: How many catfish did the fishing cat catch?

Victorian Cat

1. Make a curly V.

2. Put it on a hat.

3. Make cat ears, head...

4. and face.

5. Draw two curly whiskers and a frilly collar.

6. Make an arm in a puff sleeve...

7. and another one.

8. Draw a table...

9. teacup, teapot, and fish crumpet.

10. Add flowers to everything!

Tea and crumpets, everyone? Queen Victoria reigned from 1837 to 1901 at a time when it was said that the sun never set on the British empire. Her favorite cat was White Heather, an Angora who outlived her and was inherited by her son, King Edward VII.

Cat Fact: *Vibrissae* is the scientific word for cat whiskers, which are way different than human hair. They're like touch antennae, telling the cat lots about what's going on. So don't ever shave a cat's whiskers.

Wondercat

All cats were wild at one time, and scientists don't know exactly when or how cats first became part of the family, but it happened thousands of years ago. Now domestic cats way outnumber wild cats. Just compare the estimated 82,000,000 domestic cats in the United States to only 100 Scottish wild cats like this natural wonder.

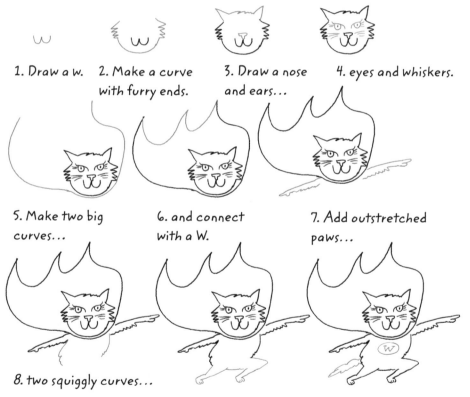

1. Draw a w.

2. Make a curve with furry ends.

3. Draw a nose and ears...

4. eyes and whiskers.

5. Make two big curves...

6. and connect with a W.

7. Add outstretched paws...

8. two squiggly curves...

9. and bent back legs.

10. Make a tail and a W.

Cat Fact: If you want to be a cool cat, whether you're wild or domestic, you have to keep yourself clean. Cats can spend up to half their waking hours grooming themselves with their built-in scrub brush tongues.

King Xerxes

 1. Draw an X.

 2. Make a head with two round ears...

 3. eyes and nose.

 4. Draw a Persian crown.

5. Make a squiggly line mane.

6. Add four curves...

Now rare, the Persian lion once reigned throughout the Middle East and India. It was a symbol of the strength and power of kings such as Xerxes and was pictured on coins, art, carpets, and buildings.

 7. two paws and another curve.

8. Draw two sides to the throne...

 9. and royal feet.

 Cat Fact: X marks the spot. The X chromosome is what determines a cat's color.

Yoga Cat

A cat on the mat is where it's at! Balance, strength, flexibility—cats are natural yoga masters. Their tails help them keep their balance.

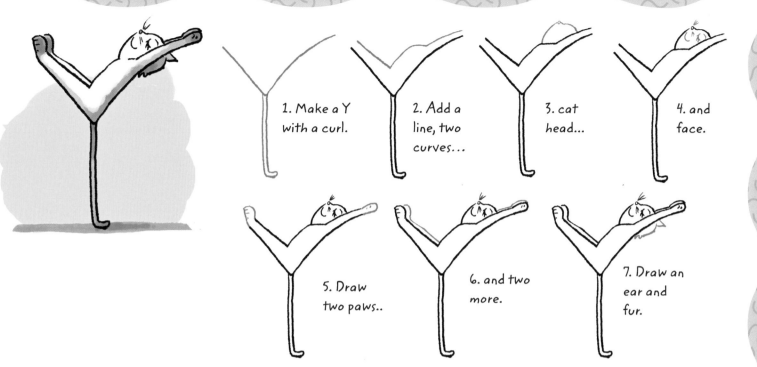

1. Make a Y with a curl.

2. Add a line, two curves...

3. cat head...

4. and face.

5. Draw two paws..

6. and two more.

7. Draw an ear and fur.

Cat Fact: Cats don't have collarbones like we do, so they can squeeze through tight spaces. If a cat can get its head through, it can get the rest of its body through, too!

Cat Zydeco

Zydeco is foot-stomping dance music from Louisiana. Like most domestic cats, it's not purebred, but a colorful mix of French Creole, African, blues, folk, and rhythm and blues.

 **Cat Fact:** No broccoli, thank you! When it comes to dinner, cats are strictly carnivores. That means meat, poultry, or fish.

1. Draw two bouncy Z's.

2. Add another Z and an S.

3. Tap your feet.

4. Draw two curves and a paw...

5. two more curves and a paw...

6. holding a box and five skinny Z's.

7. Make cat ears and cheeks...

8. and a singing cat face.

9. Swing your tail and play!

1. Draw a 1.

2. Attach three curves...

3. a leg...

4. and ear.

5. Attach two curves and nose...

6. a leg...

7. and two more legs.

8. This cat is happy to see you!

❶ Tail

Cats talk with their tails. A tail up means, "I'm happy to see you!" A cat's tail has more than 20 bones, which lets a cat make a lot of different moves to say how she really feels.

What cat tails say:

I'm happy!

I'm really happy!

I'm MAD!

I'm REALLY MAD!

I'm NOT a cat!

② Eyes

A cat needs to see in the daytime and the nighttime. What it needs to see most is movement, like a mouse running across the barn floor. It doesn't need to know what color the mouse is in order to catch it, so a cat can see when it's very dark, but can't see all the colors of the rainbow.

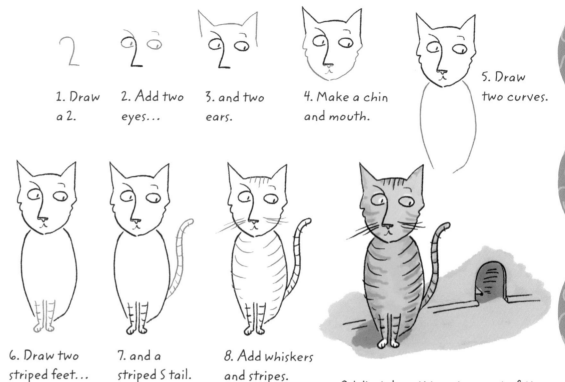

1. Draw a 2.

2. Add two eyes...

3. and two ears.

4. Make a chin and mouth.

5. Draw two curves.

6. Draw two striped feet...

7. and a striped S tail.

8. Add whiskers and stripes.

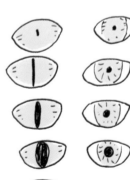

9. What does this cat see out of the corner of its eye?

Cat Fact: The black part of the eye, the pupil, opens and closes to let light in. Human pupils are round and get bigger and smaller. Cat pupils contract sideways, so when it's very bright, the cat's pupil looks like a line, and when it's dark, the cat's pupil is almost the whole eye.

Cat eye   Human eye

③ Little Kittens

These three little kittens have lost their mittens just like in the nursery rhyme. But they don't have to look for them, because you can draw each kitten a pair of brand new mittens to match its fur!

3   3   3

1. Draw three tiny 3's...

2. turn them into noses and draw six eyes...

3. and three kitten heads with ears.

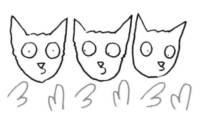

4. Make six funny 3's...

5. and turn them into three pairs of mittens.

6. Add hats to match!

Cat Fact: Squeak! Did you hear that? No? Your cat did. Though cats can't hear at all when they're first born, within just a few weeks they can hear high-pitched sounds, like mouse squeaks, that human ears don't hear.

Cat Fact: Stealth walkers! When cats walk, they place the hind paw in the track of the front paw. which makes less noise and fewer tracks.

④ Feet

How is a cat like a giraffe? It's in the way they walk! Cats and giraffes move both legs on each side at the same time. Left legs forward, right legs back. Right legs forward, left legs back. Most animals move their left front leg and back right leg at the same time, and their right front leg and back left leg at the same time.

1. Draw two tiny 4's.

2. Turn them into two legs.

3. Draw two more 4's...

4. and turn them into two legs.

5. Make four paws...

6. and a cat face...

7. with ears.

8. Make a back...

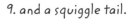

9. and a squiggle tail.

High 5

Cats have five toes on each front paw and four toes on each back paw, for a total of 18 toes—and 18 claws!

1. Draw two 5's.

2. Add six lines...

3. and two paws.

4. Draw one face and four ears.

5. Add two bent arms and paws.

6. Make two curves and two legs...

7. and two more legs.

8. Add whiskers and tails.

Kitty Quiz: What's black, orange, and fuzzy and says

MEOW!

A cat-erpillar.

6th Sense

Cats have five senses just like humans—sight, hearing, smell, touch, and taste. Their senses of hearing and smell are way better than ours. They can see better than we can in the dark, and their whiskers give them extra-sensitive touch perception. Some people think cats have a sixth sense—extra-sensory perception—that tells them when something good or bad is going to happen.

1. Draw a 6...

2. and a 0 and turn them into eyes to see.

3. Draw two ears to hear...

4. and a nose to smell.

5. Make whiskers to touch...

6. and a tongue to taste.

7. Draw a crystal ball and foretell the future.

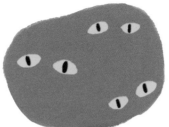

Cat Facts: Why do a cat's eyes shine at night? It's all done with mirrors! A patch of cells on the back of the cat's eye reflects light like a mirror, helping the cat to see in the dark.

1. Draw two 7's.

2. Add two squiggles and another 7.

3. Make a lucky cat face.

4. Add a curve and paw.

5. Add another curve and paw.

6. Make a curvy 7 tail.

7. Draw three 7's and...

8. turn them into legs.

7 Lucky Cat

This is one lucky cat! It's made of seven lucky number 7's, and it's about to catch a lucky falling star. While black cats have a reputation for bad luck, tortoiseshell and calico cats are considered lucky.

9. Catch a lucky falling star!

Cat Tale: Welcome to our lucky house! Maneki-neko is a Japanese lucky cat charm that people put at the entrance of their homes or shops. With a friendly wave, Maneki-neko encourages visitors to come in and share the luck.

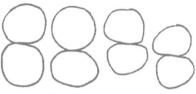

1. Draw four 8's.

2. Add sixteen ears...

3. sixteen closed eyes...

4. and eight wide open mouths!

5. Put them in a basket and give them each a name.

Litter of 8 Kittens

Kittens can't see or hear when they're born, but they sure can cry! Kittens are born with their eyes closed and ears sealed shut because they need more time to develop. They'll start to see in five to ten days and to hear in about two and a half weeks.

Cat Fact: Adopt a kitty! Eight weeks is the minimum legal age for adoption. Most cats reach adult size in about one year.

⑨ Lives

People say that cats have nine lives because they always seem to land on their feet. Cats really only have one life, which can be as long as 20 years.

1. Draw a 9.

2. Make it a terrified 9.

3. Make it a terrified cat.

4. Attach eight lines...

5. and four paws.

6. Add a tail, tall building, and...

7. open your parachute!

Want to have lunch? I'm vegetarian.

⑩ Gymnasticat

This cat scored a purrrrrfect 10 on the balance beam! Strong and graceful, cats are gymnasts of the animal world. Their backbones are extra flexible, so they can flip and turn in midair and still land on their feet.

Cat Fact: Cats speak in whiskers! The position of a cat's whiskers can tell you what she's feeling.

1. Draw a slanted 10.

2. Make a face...

3. outstretched arms...

4. paws and ears.

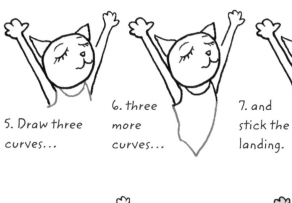

5. Draw three curves...

6. three more curves...

7. and stick the landing.

8. Tail up! Whiskers up!

9. You scored a 10!